These Thy Gifts

A Collection of Simple Meal Prayers

Mark G. Boyer

acta
PUBLICATIONS

THESE THY GIFTS
A Collection of Simple Meal Prayers
by Mark G. Boyer

Edited by Andrew Yankech
Cover design by Tom A. Wright
Text Design and typesetting by Patricia Lynch

Scripture quotations are from the *New Revised Standard Version Bible*, copyright © 1989 by the Division of Christian Education of the National Council of the Churches of Christ in the USA. Used by permission. All rights reserved.

Published by ACTA Publications, 4848 N. Clark Street, Chicago, IL 60640, (800) 397-2282, www.actapublications.com

Library of Congress Number: 2010933001
ISBN: 978-0-87946-435-6
Printed in The United States by Evangel Press
Year 17 16 15 14 13 12 11 10
Printing 10 09 08 07 06 05 04 03 02 First Edition

Contents

Dedicated to

Tyler Durham,
Master of Ceremonies,

Mitchell Dotson,
Assistant Master of Ceremonies,

and Michael Clarke and Julia Kovacs,
Altar Server Trainers,

St. Francis of Assisi Parish
Nixa, Missouri

Introduction

Bless us, O Lord,
and these thy gifts,
which we are about to receive
from thy bounty,
through Christ our Lord.
Amen.

F OR COUNTLESS CHRISTIANS, THE SIMPLE WORDS ABOVE evoke a lifetime of meals shared in love with friends and family, meals scrounged together in lean times, and feasts celebrated in times of plenty. They bring us together to enjoy the gifts that God has bestowed on us, and they remind us to be stewards of whatever God has entrusted to us. Because everything belongs to God, even the food we eat, we can do no less than thank God for what the Holy One graciously gives to us. In his letter to the Romans, St. Paul urges people to "persevere in prayer" (12:12). Likewise, he tells the Philippians that "in everything by prayer and supplication with thanksgiving" to let their "requests be made known to God" (4:6). One characteristic of the earliest Christian community as described by Luke in his Acts of the Apostles is that the members of the community "were constantly devoting themselves to prayer" (Acts 1:14).

Thus, among many people there is the custom of saying a meal prayer before eating as a sign that they are devoted to prayer, "keeping alert in it with thanksgiving" (Colossians 4:2). The ritual and tradition in reciting table grace offer comfort and ease, and that simple prayer has a powerful ability to remind people to eat in thanksgiving to God. But sometimes we can benefit from a little change from the normal to keep us alert in our faith. Indeed, the meal prayers in this book are not designed to replace the saying of grace, but simply to open our eyes to new ways of thanking God for the food set before us. And then, when we return to the prayers we've known all our lives, we can do so with renewed vigor and appreciation.

While there are other books of collections of meal prayers, they require either multiple copies of the books or sheets printed with various refrains or verses on them. *These Thy Gifts*, composed of simple meal prayers based on the Psalms and biblical canticles, requires that only the person saying the meal prayer choose one and pray it before a family sits down to share a meal.

This book presents choices of simple meal prayers that correspond to the seasons of the liturgical year. It is designed to be kept on the table or counter where it can be used for a few seconds before eating. While the prayers are phrased in the plural, they can easily be prayed by one who eats alone by turning the plurals into singulars, such as "we" to "I," "us" to "me," "our" to "my," etc.

The meal prayers for Advent focus on the two aspects of that season: the second coming of Christ in glory and his birth in history. The prayers for the season of Christmas mark Christ's birth, his Epiphany, and his Baptism, along with the other feasts of Christmas. The Lenten prayers for each Sunday and week of this penitential season echo the themes of prayer, fasting, and almsgiving which begin on Ash Wednesday and culminate on Holy Thursday, when the Easter Triduum begins. Each day of Holy Week and the Triduum has its own special meal prayers which illustrate an aspect of these special days. For each Sunday of Easter a meal prayer highlighting Christ's resurrection is presented along with choices to be used throughout the fifty days of this season. Likewise, a selection of general meal prayers is provided for the thirty-three to thirty-four weeks of Ordinary Time. For those who wish to mark the feasts and solemnities of the liturgy year, prayers are provided for all major celebrations. There is even a section of meal prayers for special days, like birthdays, anniversaries, father's day, mother's day, etc.

It is the author's hope that each meal will find more and more people uttering a prayer of thanksgiving for the food and drink God sets before them.

The Season
of Advent

Your promises, O Lord, are pure;
they are like silver refined in a furnace
and seven times purified.
Protect us and guard us.
Bless this food and drink we share.
We await the coming of our Savior, Jesus Christ. Amen.

O Lord, our chosen portion and cup,
you hold our lot in your hands.
We bless you for your counsel.
Make our hearts glad
and make our souls rejoice
as we prepare to welcome your Son,
Jesus Christ, who is Lord forever and ever. Amen.

WE LOVE YOU, O LORD, OUR STRENGTH.
You are our rock, our fortress, our deliverer.
As we prepare to celebrate the incarnation of your Son,
grant that we may take refuge in your strength.
We call upon you to bless our food and drink.
May our eating and drinking serve as praise of you,
who lives and reigns as one God,
Father, Son, and Holy Spirit, forever and ever. Amen.

O LORD,
do not be far away from us.
When in need, come quickly to our aid.
Deliver us from all that hinders us
from welcoming the Savior with joy.
Bless this Advent food and drink
that helps us prepare for the birth of Jesus Christ,
who lives and reigns with you and the Holy Spirit,
one God forever and ever. Amen.

WE LIFT UP OUR HEADS, O GOD.
We open up the doors of our hearts, O Lord.
We await the coming of the king of glory,
your son, Jesus Christ.
May this Advent meal serve
to prepare us for his arrival.
Hear us through the same Christ our Lord. Amen.

O LORD,
we believe that we shall see your goodness
in the land of the living.
During this Advent season, we wait for you.
Through this food and drink,
make us strong and let our hearts take courage.
Help us to prepare to celebrate the birth of your son,
Jesus Christ, who is Lord forever and ever. Amen.

O GOD, CONTINUE YOUR STEADFAST LOVE
to those who know you
and your salvation to the true of heart.
As we prepare to celebrate the birth of your son,
let us drink from the river of your delights.
You are the fountain of life,
and in your light we see the coming of the true Light,
Jesus Christ, who is Lord forever and ever. Amen.

WE PLACE ALL OUR TRUST IN YOU, O LORD.
We take delight in you
and hope that you will give us the desires of our hearts.
As we prepare to eat this Advent meal,
we still ourselves in your presence
and we wait patiently for the coming of our Savior,
Jesus Christ, who lives with you and the Holy Spirit,
one God, forever and ever. Amen.

O LORD, YOU KNOW OUR DAYS AND YEARS.
Our steps are made firm by you.
When we stumble, you hold us by the hand.
During this Advent season,
we seek your blessing upon our food and drink.
May these gifts strengthen us
as we wait in joyful hope
for the coming of our Savior, Jesus Christ. Amen.

YOU KNOW ALL OUR LONGINGS, O LORD.
Our sighing is not hidden from you.
Our hearts throb, our strength fails us,
our eyesight leaves us.
But it is for your Son, O Lord, that we wait.
We know that he will come and answer and not delay.
Make our Advent waiting holy,
and bless our food and drink.
Hear us through Christ our Lord. Amen.

W E ARE WAITING PATIENTLY FOR YOU, O LORD.
Incline your head to us and hear our cry.
Through our Advent observance,
draw us up from the desolate pit of materialism
and set our feet upon the rock of righteousness.
Put a new song in our mouths,
that we may praise you for this food and drink.
We put all our trust in you,
through Jesus Christ our Lord. Amen.

G IVE EAR TO OUR PRAYER, O GOD,
and do not hide yourself from our supplication.
Attend to us and answer our Advent prayer.
Through the nourishment of this food and drink,
grant that we may be found worthy
to welcome Christ in glory,
for he is Lord forever and ever. Amen.

G OD, YOU LISTEN TO THE PLEAS AND SUPPLICATIONS
OF ALL THE WORLD,
and you hear and answer those who call to you.
We send our burdens up to you,
trusting that you will sustain us
through your blessing of our food and drink.
Keep us steadfast in your love
as we wait in joyful hope
for the coming of our Savior, Jesus Christ. Amen.

R OUSE YOURSELF, O LORD GOD;
come to our help and see us.
We keep watch for your coming
throughout this season of Advent.
Help us to know your steadfast love
and bless this food and drink,
gifts from your hand.
Hear us through Christ our Lord. Amen.

O GOD, WE AWAIT YOU IN SILENCE.
From you comes salvation,
for you alone are our rock and our fortress.
May our Advent observance
prepare us to welcome Christ when he comes in glory.
May your blessing upon this meal
prepare us to praise you, eternal Trinity:
Father, Son, and Holy Spirit, one God
forever and ever. Amen.

OUR GOD AND KING,
You work salvation on the earth.
You divide the sea by your might.
You cut openings for springs and torrents.
Yours is the day and yours is the night.
You have fixed all the bounds of the earth.
You made summer and fall, winter and spring.
As we await the coming of your Son, Jesus Christ,
shine your light upon us
and bless this food that comes from you. Amen.

O LORD, ON THE HOLY MOUNTAIN
stands the city you founded—Jerusalem.
Glorious things are spoken of the place
where you chose to live among your people.
During this Advent season we await the new Jerusalem
where Christ will return
to judge the living and the dead.
Bless this food and use it to strengthen us,
as we wait in joyful hope for the coming
of our Savior, Jesus Christ. Amen.

O LORD, WE CRY OUT TO YOU IN THE MORNING.
We pray to you in the evening.
We have seen your face in the person of your Son.
As we prepare to celebrate his birth,
bless this Advent food and drink.
Keep us faithful as we await
the coming of Christ in glory,
for he is Lord forever and ever. Amen.

WE SING TO YOU A NEW SONG, O LORD,
for you have done wondrous things.
You have remembered your steadfast love
and faithfulness
by bringing to birth your son, Jesus Christ.
All the ends of the earth have seen your victory.
As we prepare for his coming,
bless this Advent food and drink
through the same Christ our Lord. Amen.

WE LIFT UP OUR EYES TO YOU, O LORD;
from you will come our help.
You neither sleep nor linger,
but keep us in your steadfast love.
Guard our goings out and our comings in,
keep us from all evil,
and bless this food we share,
as we await the coming of our Savior, Jesus Christ.
Amen.

B LESSED BE YOUR NAME, O LORD,
creator of heaven and earth.
We place all our trust in you.
Grant peace to this house
and all who live here.
May this Advent food prepare us for the coming
of our Lord Jesus Christ. Amen.

O LORD, YOUR SON, JESUS CHRIST, EMPTIED HIMSELF
and took the form of a servant
in order to save the world.
As we prepare to celebrate his birth,
bless this food and drink.
May it give us strength to be followers of him,
who lives and reigns with you and the Holy Spirit,
one God, forever and ever. Amen.

O LORD, ALL YOUR WORKS BLESS YOU;
they praise and exalt you above all forever.
We praise your name
as we prepare to celebrate the birth of Jesus.
May this food and drink make us ready
to welcome him when he comes in glory.
We bless you, Father, Son, and Holy Spirit, forever and
ever. Amen.

O LORD OUR GOD, YOU ARE WORTHY
O Lord our God, you are worthy
to receive glory and honor and power.
You have created all things,
and you give food and drink to all your creatures.
Bless our Advent preparation
that we may celebrate the birth of Christ with joy.
Amen.

I NVISIBLE GOD AND FATHER OF JESUS,
you revealed your face in the image of your son.
As we prepare to celebrate his birth,
bless our food and drink.
Grant that the sharing at our table
will give you thanks forever and ever. Amen.

I N THE PEACE OF THIS ADVENT SEASON,
we come to you in prayer, O Lord.
Grant that your people
may beat their swords into plowshares
and their spears into pruning hooks
that the world will have enough food to eat
and less war to support with costly weapons.
Grant your blessing upon this food,
that it may enable us to walk in your light.
We ask this through Christ our Lord. Amen.

O LORD, OUR SOULS YEARN FOR YOU.
We use this Advent season to keep vigil.
As we prepare for the coming of your Son,
grant us the peace of this season.
May your blessing come upon our food and drink
that we may put all our trust in you.
Hear us through Christ our Lord.
Amen.

The Season
of Christmas

W E HAVE KEPT YOUR WAYS, O GOD,
and we have waited for the birth of your son.
As we celebrate his incarnation,
you light up our darkness with his truth.
Bless our Christmas food and drink
that will enable us to serve you ever more faithfully
through Jesus Christ our Lord. Amen.

A LL OF THE HEAVENS PROCLAIM YOUR GLORY, O GOD,
at the birth of your only-begotten son.
The sun sings your glory throughout the universe
as it rises and sets.
Bless this food and drink
as we celebrate the incarnation.
May we, too, sing your praises:
Glory to you, Father, Son, and Holy Spirit,
one God, worthy of all praise forever and ever. Amen.

Mighty Lord,
we join with the angels in praising you
for the birth of Jesus, our Savior and Lord.
We proclaim this good news to our sisters and brothers.
We stand in awe of you
as we share this Christmas food and drink.
Bless these gifts and all who gather at this table.
Praise to you Lord forever and ever. Amen.

O Lord, we love the house in which you dwell
and the place where your glory abides.
At the birth of your son
we come singing a song of thanksgiving
and telling all your wondrous deeds.
Grant us redemption through our Christmas meal
that acknowledges your graciousness to us.
Hear our praise through Christ our Lord. Amen.

C OME AND HEAR, ALL YOU WHO WORSHIP GOD,
and we will tell what he has done for us.
We cried aloud to God and he heard our prayer.
He has listened and sent us a Savior.
May our observance of Jesus' birth
through our sharing of this food and drink
be accepted as praise in your sight, O God.
We ask this through Christ our Lord. Amen.

O GOD, YOU HAVE BEEN GRACIOUS AND BLESSED US;
you have made your face to shine upon us
in the person of your son, Jesus Christ.
He has made known your ways to us.
Through this celebration of his birth
and this food and drink you give us,
may all people praise you
through the same Christ our Lord. Amen.

O GOD, LET ALL THE PEOPLES PRAISE YOU
for the gift of our Savior, Jesus Christ.
Let all the nations be glad and sing for joy
because you guide us in your ways through him.
Raise your hand in blessing upon this Christmas meal.
Let all the peoples praise you, O God,
through Christ our Lord. Amen.

WE GIVE THANKS TO YOU, O GOD;
we give thanks for you are near.
You have revealed your glory
through the birth of your son, Jesus Christ.
As we celebrate his incarnation,
let this food and drink
and the collection of people around this table
be holy in your sight.
We rejoice forever and sing you praise
through the same Jesus Christ our Lord. Amen.

O LORD, GOD OF ALL,
   your son's birth is your gift to us.
Bless the food and drink
which we will use to celebrate this Christmas feast.
Help us to seek your name
for you are the Lord, the Most High over all the earth,
forever and ever. Amen.

O LORD OF ALL THE WORLD,
   you chose to dwell among us
in the person of your only-begotten son, Jesus Christ.
Hear our prayer and give ear to our pleas
to bless this Christmas meal.
Through our food and drink,
bestow upon us your blessings
through the same Christ our Lord. Amen.

W̶E COME SINGING TO YOU, O LORD.
We make a joyful noise to you,
the rock of our salvation,
as we celebrate these days of Christmas.
We come into your presence with thanksgiving
for this food and drink and those around this table.
You are the great God whom we praise
through Jesus Christ our Lord. Amen.

W̶E COME IN WORSHIP AND BOW DOWN
BEFORE YOU, O LORD.
We kneel before the manger of our Maker.
We are your people and the sheep of your pasture.
Today hear our prayer of praise
and listen to our songs of gratitude
as we celebrate the birth of Jesus Christ, your son,
who lives and reigns with you and the Holy Spirit,
one God forever and ever. Amen.

WE SING TO YOU, O LORD, A NEW SONG.
We sing to you, O Lord, and bless your name.
We tell of the salvation that comes from you
as we celebrate the incarnation
of Jesus Christ, your son.
Through him, your glory has been revealed
to all the nations.
Bless this food and drink, gifts from your hand,
for you are great and greatly to be praised
through Christ our Lord. Amen.

WE ASCRIBE GLORY AND STRENGTH TO YOU, O LORD,
as we celebrate the birth of your son.
We worship you in holy splendor
and ask your blessing upon this food and drink.
Hear our prayer through the same Christ our Lord.
Amen.

THE HEAVENS ARE GLAD
AND THE EARTH REJOICES, O LORD,
at the birth of your only-begotten son
from the Virgin Mary.
The seas roar, the fields exult,
and trees sing for joy before you,
for Christ has come to judge the earth.
Grant that his judgment of righteousness and truth
will find us acceptable in your sight.
May this Christmas food and drink give your praise
through the same Christ our Lord. Amen.

YOU HAVE DONE GREAT THINGS FOR US, O LORD,
and we rejoice in your holy name.
As we share the peace of this Christmas season,
make this food and drink holy in your sight.
We come before you with shouts of joy
as we celebrate the birth of your son, Jesus Christ,
who is Lord forever and ever. Amen.

OUR EYES ARE TURNED TOWARD YOU, O GOD.
We have seen your salvation offered to all people
through the incarnation of your son, Jesus Christ.
You have dealt bountifully with us,
providing this food and drink
and the warm company gathered around this table.
All thanks be to you throughout this Christmas season
through Jesus Christ in the unity of the Holy Spirit,
one God, forever and ever. Amen.

O LORD, WE OFFER THIS PRAYER TO YOU.
You are great and glorious,
wonderful in power and unsurpassable.
All your creatures serve you.
Bless this Christmas meal that comes from your hand
that it may strengthen us in your service.
You are Father, Son, and Holy Spirit,
one God, forever and ever. Amen.

FATHER OF OUR LORD JESUS CHRIST,
you have made us worthy
to share the fate of the saints in light.
You have rescued us from the power of darkness
and brought us into your kingdom
through the birth
of your only-begotten son, Jesus Christ.
Bless this food and drink,
and accept our thanks and praise
through the same Christ our Lord. Amen.

O GOD, YOU COVERED THE HEAVENS IN GLORY
and filled the earth with praise
at the birth of your son, Jesus Christ,
who came forth to save us.
Fill us with the splendor of his light,
and, through your blessing upon our food,
enable us to rejoice and exult in you forever and ever.
Amen.

W E SING TO YOU A NEW SONG, O LORD.
From one end of the earth to another,
we praise your name.
Through the incarnation of your son,
you have turned darkness into light,
you have made crooked ways straight.
May your blessing upon this Christmas food
fortify us to walk always in your ways
through Jesus Christ our Lord,
who lives and reigns with you and the Holy Spirit,
one God, forever and ever. Amen.

W E PRAISE YOU, LORD, FOR ALL YOUR GOODNESS.
We bless you, King of the Ages,
for all you have done.
The bright light of your son's birth
has shone on all parts of the earth.
People are drawn to him by your name, O Lord.
We join with other generations
to ask your blessing upon this food and drink.
We give joyful praise for your Chosen One,
Jesus Christ, who is Lord forever and ever. Amen.

O CHRIST, YOU WERE MANIFESTED IN THE FLESH
and justified in the Spirit.
You were contemplated by the angels
and proclaimed by the pagans.
You are believed in the world
and exalted in glory.
Bless this Christmas feast
and all gathered at this table. Amen.

The Season
of Lent

Ash Wednesday

O Lord, we begin this season of repentance
with the cross of death
smeared in ashes on our heads.
We will afflict ourselves with fasting.
We will pray with our heads bowed.
We will give to those who ask of us.
Make holy these forty days and bless our food.
Hear us through Christ our Lord. Amen.

O Lord, creator of all life,
you turn us back to dust at the end of our lives.
A thousand years in your sight are like yesterday
when it is past, or like a watch in the night.
Have compassion on your servants
as we begin this Lenten season.
Satisfy us with your steadfast love
so that we may rejoice and be glad all our days.
Bless this meager meal we share
and lead us through Lent to Easter joy.
We ask this through Christ our Lord. Amen.

Lenten Days

HAVE MERCY ON US, O GOD,
according to your steadfast love.
According to your abundant mercy,
blot out our transgressions.
Wash us thoroughly from our iniquity
and cleanse us from our sins.
Work repentance in us throughout this Lent.
Bless this meager food and the fasting
that accompanies it.
Hear us through Christ our Lord. Amen.

ANSWER US WHEN WE CALL, O GOD.
Be gracious to us, and hear our prayer.
Strengthen us in our fasting
even as you bless this meager food.
Hear us through Christ our Lord. Amen.

WHEN WE ARE DISTURBED, O LORD,
you urge us to pray and to be silent
and to ponder your words.
During this time of abstinence,
bless our sacrifice
and strengthen us in your service.
We ask this through Christ our Lord. Amen.

O LORD,
during this time of repentance,
we take refuge in you.
Spread your protection over us
for the sake of your name which we love.
Bless the food we share
for the sake of your son, Jesus Christ,
who suffered and died for us.
He is Lord forever and ever. Amen.

S TEADFAST AND LOVING LORD,
turn toward us and save our lives.
Make our Lenten discipline
of prayer, fasting, and almsgiving
a means for us to return to you.
May this prayer bring your blessing to us
through Jesus Christ our Lord. Amen.

W E GIVE YOU, LORD,
the thanks due your righteousness.
We sing praise to your name, Lord Most High.
Through our Lenten observance,
you bring about repentance in us.
Bless this food that strengthens us
to continue our Lenten journey to you.
Hear us through Jesus Christ our Lord. Amen.

L ORD, YOU ARE A STRONGHOLD FOR THE OPPRESSED,
a fortress in times of trouble.
Those who know your name put their trust in you
and you do not forsake those who seek you.
Strengthen us during this season of repentance
through the food we are about to share.
May we grow ever more in trust of you
through Jesus Christ our Lord. Amen.

R ISE UP, O LORD.
Rally your people
through prayer, fasting, and almsgiving.
Let us not forget the needy and the poor.
Make our Lenten penance acceptable to you,
and bless this food through Christ our Lord.
Amen.

H OW LONG, O LORD?
Will you forget us forever?
How long will you hide your face from us?
During this Lent we are turned to repentance.
Consider and answer us
as we invoke your blessing upon this meal
that comes from your bountiful hand.
We pray through Christ our Lord. Amen.

A LL-KNOWING LORD,
it is easy to get caught up
with evildoers and troublemakers.
Bring about conversion in us
and help us to know the errors of our ways.
Through your blessing upon us and this food,
give us the grace to make this Lent
a time of repentance and reform. Amen.

W E CALL UPON YOU, O GOD;
incline your ear to us and hear our words.
We confess our sins to you
during this time of repentance.
May our fasting turn our hearts
toward your steadfast love.
May your blessing upon our food
fortify us to hold fast to your ways. Amen.

G UARD US AS THE APPLE OF YOUR EYE, O LORD.
Hide us in the shadow of your wings
from those who would lead us to sin.
Through our Lenten prayer, fasting, and almsgiving
give us the strength to resist temptation.
Bless this food we share through Christ our Lord. Amen.

L ORD GOD,
    you answer us in times of trouble
by sending us the gift of the Holy Spirit.
Remember our offerings of prayer,
grant favor to our almsgiving,
and bless our fasting during this Lent.
Through our sharing of this food
may your name be praised now and forever. Amen.

O GOD, WHY HAVE YOU FORSAKEN US?
    We cry by day and by night
for forgiveness of our sins.
Through our Lenten prayer, almsgiving, and fasting,
help us to recognize your presence
and trust more deeply in your loving kindness.
Bless this food and drink
which strengthens us to do your will
through Jesus Christ our Lord. Amen.

O GOD, DURING THIS LENT
YOU POUR US OUT LIKE WATER
and jar loose our bones through prayer,
almsgiving, and fasting.
Our hearts have become like wax,
melting within our breasts.
Reshape them according to your will,
that we may be found converted in your sight
and ready to celebrate the resurrection of Jesus Christ,
who is Lord forever and ever. Amen.

A LL THE ENDS OF THE EARTH REMEMBER YOUR DEEDS
and turn to you, O Lord,
during this time of repentance.
We pray that all people will come to know you
and worship you
and that future generations will be told about you,
that they may proclaim your works
to a people yet unborn.
Bless our Lenten food and drink
through Christ our Lord. Amen.

THE EARTH AND ALL THAT IS IN IT
BELONGS TO YOU, O LORD.
You created it with its oceans and rivers
and gave it to us to live in.
How can we stand in your presence
unless you purify our hearts?
Use our Lenten prayer, fasting, and almsgiving
to make us acceptable to you.
Bless this meager meal as we seek your face, O God.
Hear us through Christ our Lord. Amen.

To you, O Lord, we lift up our souls.
O God, in you we trust.
Do not let us be put to shame.
Make us know your ways and teach us your paths
through our Lenten prayer.
Lead us in your truth and teach us
through our Lenten fasting.
Help us see the poor and suffering in our midst
through our Lenten almsgiving.
O God of our salvation,
send your blessing upon this food
and all who have gathered here.
We wait for you to hear us
through Jesus Christ our Lord. Amen.

B E MINDFUL OF YOUR MERCY, O LORD,
and do not forget your steadfast love.
Do not remember the sins of our youth
but grant us repentance through the disciplines of Lent.
Instruct us sinners in your way
and lead us to what is right.
May your blessing upon this food and drink
help us in our Lenten pilgrimage to you.
We ask this through Christ our Lord. Amen.

F OR YOUR NAME'S SAKE, O LORD,
pardon our guilt, for it is great.
Turn to us and be gracious to us.
May our Lenten prayer, fasting, and almsgiving
make us aware of the forgiveness you give.
As we share these gifts from your bounty,
guard our lives and deliver us
through Jesus Christ our Lord. Amen.

H EAR US, O LORD, WHEN WE CRY ALOUD.
Be gracious and answer us
during this Lenten season.
Hide not your face from us.
Teach us your ways through
prayer, fasting, and almsgiving.
Bless this food and drink,
and prepare us to celebrate
the resurrection of your son,
Jesus Christ, who is Lord forever and ever. Amen.

O LORD, WE ARE HAPPY
because you forgive our transgressions,
you cover our sins with your loving kindness.
Bless this Lenten meal
and make our Lenten prayer, fasting, and almsgiving
acceptable in your sight.
May our penance guide us closer to you
so that we may be found without deceit.
We ask this through Christ our Lord. Amen.

O LORD, WE ACKNOWLEDGE OUR SINS TO YOU,
and you forgive our guilt.
Grant that our Lenten disciplines
may serve to curb our stubbornness
and strengthen our trust in you.
Bless this food
and use it to draw us closer to you,
through Jesus Christ our Lord. Amen.

TRANSGRESSION SPEAKS TO US SINNERS
deep in our hearts, O Lord.
We flatter ourselves in our own iniquity.
Our words are mischief and deceit.
Through our Lenten prayer, fasting, and almsgiving,
enable us to act wisely and do good
that we might be found acceptable in your sight.
Bless this food we share
through Jesus Christ our Lord. Amen.

O LORD, BE GRACIOUS TO US AND HEAL US
for we have sinned against you.
Turn our Lenten prayer, fasting, and almsgiving
into repentance, that we may serve you
in lasting fidelity and integrity.
Bless our food and raise us up.
We ask this through Christ our Lord. Amen.

O GOD, CREATE IN US CLEAN HEARTS,
and put into us a new and righteous spirit.
Make our Lenten prayer, fasting, and almsgiving
acceptable in your sight
and a means to obtain your mercy and love.
Hide your face from our sins
and let us hear joy and gladness
as we eat this meager meal before you.
We ask this through Christ our Lord. Amen.

O GOD OF OUR SALVATION,
we praise you for delivering us from all our sins.
May our Lenten prayer, fasting, and almsgiving
serve to show you our contrite hearts.
You open our lips and our mouths declare your praise
for this food and drink you set before us.
All glory is yours through Christ our Lord. Amen.

S AVE US, O LORD, BY YOUR NAME,
and vindicate us by your might.
Hear our prayer and give ear
to the words of our mouths.
You are our helper.
You uphold our lives
through the food and drink you set before us.
Accept our Lenten sacrifice of fasting
as we give thanks to you,
O Lord, forever and ever. Amen.

B E MERCIFUL TO US, O GOD, BE MERCIFUL TO US.
In you our souls take refuge;
in the shadow of your wings we take refuge.
During this time of repentance,
we cry to you, God Most High,
that you may fulfill your purpose in us.
Through your blessing upon our food and drink,
help us to know your steadfast love and faithfulness.
We ask this through Jesus Christ our Lord. Amen.

D ELIVER US FROM OUR SINS, O GOD.
Protect us from all the evil
that can rise up against us.
May our Lenten prayer, fasting, and almsgiving
enable us to renounce all sin
and to grow in holiness in your sight.
Bless this meal that strengthens us
through Christ our Lord. Amen.

L ORD GOD, YOU ARE OUR REFUGE
during this time of prayer, fasting, and almsgiving.
Hold us by your right hand,
guide us with your counsel,
and receive us with honor.
May this food strengthen our hearts
and draw us ever closer to you.
We ask this through Jesus Christ our Lord. Amen.

O GOD, DO NOT KEEP SILENT;
do not hold your peace or be still.
Answer our prayer for your presence.
Use our Lenten fasting
to make us aware of others' hunger.
Use our Lenten almsgiving
to make us aware of other's needs.
Use our Lenten prayer
to make us aware of our dependence upon you.
Bless this food which we share
through Christ our Lord. Amen.

O LORD, YOU FORGIVE INIQUITY AND PARDON SIN.
We have sinned against you and each other.
Restore us again to your salvation
through our Lenten prayer, fasting, and almsgiving.
You show us your steadfast love
through this food that we are about to share.
Grant us your salvation through Christ our Lord.
Amen.

I NCLINE YOUR EAR, O LORD, AND ANSWER US.
We are poor and needy.
Through this food and drink,
preserve our lives, for we are devoted to you.
Through this Lenten observance,
save us, your servants, who trust in you.
You are our God.
Be gracious to us and hear our prayer
through Jesus Christ our Lord. Amen.

O LORD, YOU GLADDEN THE SOULS OF YOUR SERVANTS,
you are good and forgiving,
you abound in steadfast love.
Hear our Lenten prayer,
bless this food,
and count us among those
found favorable in your sight.
We ask this through Christ our Lord. Amen.

O LORD, WE BOW DOWN BEFORE YOU
and we glorify your name,
for you alone are God.
From the beginning of time,
you are great and have done wondrous things.
Use this food we share to teach us your ways,
that we may walk in your truth this Lent.
We give thanks to you, O Lord, with our whole hearts
through Christ our Lord. Amen.

O LORD, GOD OF OUR SALVATION,
when we cry out in your presence,
let our prayer come before you;
incline your ear to our pleas.
Bless this Lenten meal
and draw us ever closer to you
through the disciplines of this season.
We ask this through Christ our Lord. Amen.

E VERY DAY WE CALL ON YOU, O LORD.
We spread out our hands to you
during this Lenten season.
See our repentance and turn us to you.
Guide our prayer, fasting, and almsgiving
and bless this meal which comes
from your gracious bounty.
We pray through Christ our Lord. Amen.

O LORD, GOD OF ALL,
    during this season of repentance
we remember that you cut short our days
and cover us with shame for all our sins.
Remember how short our years really are
and shower us with your steadfast love.
May our Lenten prayer, fasting, and almsgiving
make us acceptable in your sight.
Blessed may you be, O Lord, forever and ever. Amen.

MERCIFUL AND GRACIOUS LORD,
    you are slow to anger
and abounding in steadfast love.
We thank you for not dealing with
us according to our sins.
We praise you for your compassion,
and we trust that you remove our transgressions.
Bless this food that we are about to receive
from the storehouse of your bounty
through Christ our Lord. Amen.

GOOD AND FORGIVING GOD,
we and our ancestors have sinned.
We have committed iniquity
and forgotten our Savior.
During this time of repentance
bring us back to you.
Deliver us from our own foolishness.
Remember us for the sake of your covenant
and show compassion according to the abundance
of your steadfast love.
Bless this food and drink
that we may give thanks to your holy name
forever and ever. Amen.

O LORD, YOU TEACH US THE WAY OF YOUR STATUTES
so that we can observe them
to the end of our days.
Give us understanding, that we may keep your law
and observe it with all our hearts.
Lead us in the path of your commandments
and bless this meager food and drink we share,
that we may make our way through Lent
with prayer, fasting, and almsgiving
that draw us ever closer to you.
We ask this through Christ our Lord. Amen

YOUR HANDS MADE AND FASHIONED US, O LORD.
As we prepare to eat this meal,
give us understanding that we may learn your ways.
Let your steadfast love become our comfort.
Let your mercy come to us that we may live.
Through our Lenten observance
make our hearts blameless in your sight.
All praise to you forever and ever. Amen.

WITH OUR WHOLE HEARTS WE CRY TO YOU, O LORD;
in your great mercy answer us.
We rise at dawn and cry for help.
We go to bed at night seeking your salvation.
In your steadfast love hear our prayer
and bless this meal that you set before us.
As we eat it, let us meditate on your promise
that we may grow in your grace this Lent
through Jesus Christ our Lord. Amen.

GREAT IS YOUR MERCY, O LORD.
Great is your love.
Accept our Lenten prayer, fasting, and almsgiving,
and bless this meager meal that will sustain us.
May we know more deeply the truth of your word
through Jesus Christ our Lord. Amen.

LET OUR CRIES COME BEFORE YOU, O LORD,
give us understanding according to your word.
Let our supplication come before you;
deliver us according to your promise.
With our lips we pour forth praise to you
for all the many gifts you have given to us,
especially this food and drink.
During this Lent, we long for your salvation.
Grant us new life in Christ,
who is Lord forever and ever. Amen.

HAVE MERCY UPON US, O LORD.
Have mercy upon us,
for we have had more than enough of contempt.
Use our Lenten prayer, fasting, and almsgiving
to focus our eyes on you and your great mercy.
We ask your blessing upon this food
we are about to share
through Jesus Christ our Lord. Amen.

Out of the depths we cry to you, O Lord.
Hear our voices;
let your ears be attentive to our supplications.
Through our Lenten prayer, fasting, and almsgiving,
help us to know your forgiveness.
As we wait in hope for your word,
bless this food and drink.
We pray through Christ our Lord. Amen.

O Lord, you search us and know us.
You know when we sit and when we stand;
you discern our thoughts from far away.
Even before a word is on our tongues you know it.
Direct our Lenten path in your ways
so that our prayer, fasting, and almsgiving
may bring us closer to you
and all the peoples of the earth.
Send your blessing upon this meal
which we eat before you.
We pray through Christ our Lord. Amen.

B LESSED AND PRAISEWORTHY ARE YOU, O LORD,
and glorious forever is your name.
We have sinned and transgressed.
With contrite heart and humble spirit
receive our Lenten penitence
that we may follow you with our whole hearts.
Bless this meal through Jesus Christ our Lord. Amen.

O LORD, YOUR CHRIST SUFFERED FOR US
and left us an example
for us follow in his footsteps.
Use our Lenten prayer, fasting, and almsgiving
to help us carry our crosses.
Through your blessing upon this food
grant that we may follow Christ into death
and come to share in his resurrection.
We ask this through the same Christ our Lord. Amen.

Holy Week
and Easter Triduum

Palm Sunday of the Lord's Passion

B LESSED ARE YOU, O CHRIST, FOR YOU COME
in the name of the Lord.

The festive procession with palm branches blesses you.

You, the stone that the builders rejected,

have become the chief cornerstone of your Church.

This is God's doing,

and it is marvelous in our eyes.

Save us, we beseech you, O Christ,

through this food and drink

that we use to honor your passion.

You live and reign with the Father and the Holy Spirit,

one God forever and ever. Amen.

O GOD, YOUR LOVE IS STEADFAST.
We place our all hope in you.
We have followed your son in procession
to your house amid glad shouts
and songs of thanksgiving.
And we have kept vigil
as he suffered and died on the cross.
May our observance of this Palm Sunday
and the food and drink we share
strengthen us to follow him in his passion.
He is Lord forever and ever. Amen.

MONDAY OF HOLY WEEK

O LORD, YOU ARE THE GOD WHO GIVES US LIGHT.
We give thanks to you for you are good
and your steadfast love endures forever.
Make us grateful for all the gifts you share with us,
especially this food and drink.
Make this week holy,
as we prepare to celebrate the death and resurrection
of Jesus Christ, your Son, who is Lord forever and ever.
Amen.

Tuesday of Holy Week

O LORD, WE PRAISE YOU WITH UPRIGHT HEARTS.
Keep us blameless in your sight
as you give us the wisdom to walk in your ways.
May this food and drink help us to keep your word.
May this food and drink enable us
to seek you with all our hearts.
Blessed are you, O Lord, forever and ever. Amen.

Wednesday of Holy Week

O LORD, YOU DEAL BOUNTIFULLY WITH US,
so that we may live and observe your word.
Open our eyes that we may behold
all the wondrous things you do for us.
Make us long for you
as we meditate upon the suffering
and death of your son,
Jesus Christ, who lives and reigns with you
and the Holy Spirit, one God, forever and ever. Amen.

Easter Triduum
Holy Thursday

GOD OF MIGHTY WORKS,
you split open the rock in the wilderness
and it gushed with flowing water.
You opened the heavens
and rained down manna.
On the wings of the wind
quail descended in the desert.
On the night before he died,
your son, Jesus Christ, spread the table
with the feast of his body and blood.
May this Holy Thursday meal
make us grateful for all your glorious deeds.
Your hand feeds us and you answer all our needs
through Jesus Christ our Lord. Amen.

Good Friday

O SHEPHERD OF ISRAEL,
    you guide your people in your ways;
you hear our cries and you come to save us.
As the One you made strong for yourself
hung in death on the cross,
you raised him to your right hand.
Through him you have restored us;
through him your light shines upon us.
May this meager food and drink we share
in honor of Christ's death and resurrection
strengthen us in your service.
Hear us through the same Christ our Lord. Amen.

Holy Saturday

O LORD OUR GOD,
 you brought our ancestors out of Egypt
into a land flowing with milk and honey.
In the fullness of time, you brought us
out of the land of sin
into a home with a table filled with the finest wheat.
As we prepare to celebrate the resurrection of your son,
who gives us his body and blood as food and drink,
bless this meal we set before you.
We sing aloud to you and shout for joy to you.
Hear our praise and thanksgiving
through Jesus Christ our Lord. Amen.

O LORD, THE EARTH TREMBLED AT YOUR PRESENCE
   as you led your chosen people out of Egypt.
The sea looked and fled;
the Jordan River turned back on its course.
Even the mountains and hills skipped like lambs.
You have turned the rock of Jesus' death
into the pool of water of his resurrection
and given us to eat and drink of his new life.
Bless this food which will enable us to celebrate Easter.
We ask this through Christ our Lord. Amen.

Easter Sunday

W̲E̲ ̲G̲I̲V̲E̲ ̲T̲H̲A̲N̲K̲S̲ ̲T̲O̲ ̲Y̲O̲U̲,̲ O Lord,
for you are good.
Your steadfast love endures forever.
When your only-begotten son slept in death,
you redeemed him through the power
of your Holy Spirit.
From east and west, from north and south
you have created for yourself a people
and filled them with new life.
As we celebrate the resurrection of Christ,
bless this food and drink
that sustains us now and into eternal life.
We ask this through Christ our Lord. Amen.

The Season
of Easter

LET THE LIGHT OF YOUR FACE SHINE UPON US, O LORD.
You have put Easter gladness in our hearts
greater than when the grain and wine abound.
Bless our feasting and bless our time together.
We ask this in the name of the Risen One,
Jesus Christ, our Lord. Amen.

O LORD, OUR GOD,
your name is majestic over all the earth.
By raising Jesus from the dead,
you have set your glory above the heavens.
When we look at the world and the universe around us,
we are mindful of how small we are.
Send your Easter blessing upon this food
that we may praise your sovereign name forever,
through Christ our Lord. Amen.

C REATING GOD,
to people you have given dominion
over the works of your hands.
Under our feet you have put
the beasts of the field, the birds of the air,
the fish of the sea.
Grant us a greater respect for the food you give
that we may never cease to thank you
through the risen Christ, who is Lord forever and ever.
Amen.

W E GIVE THANKS TO YOU, O LORD,
with our whole hearts
for raising Jesus from the dead
and enthroning him at your right hand in glory.
May this food that we are about to eat
strengthen us to tell more of your wonderful deeds
as we sing your praises forever
through Christ our Lord. Amen.

O LORD, YOU ARE IN YOUR HOLY PLACE.
You are enthroned in heaven.
Your eyes behold the entire world.
You love the righteous deeds of your people
and promise everlasting life
to those who follow your way.
We ask your blessing upon our food and drink,
on those around this table,
and upon those who are unable to join us today.
We make this prayer in the name of the Risen One,
Jesus Christ our Lord. Amen.

YOU SHOW US THE PATH OF LIFE, O LORD.
In your presence there is fullness of joy.
Bless us, our food, and our drink.
As we celebrate the resurrection of Christ,
may we find at your right hand pleasures forevermore.
We pray through Christ our Lord. Amen.

A T THE RESURRECTION OF YOUR SON, O LORD,
the earth reeled and rocked,
the foundations of the mountains trembled.
Out of the darkness of death
you have brought the brightness of new life.
Reaching down from heaven
you have drawn us out
of the mighty waters of baptism.
May this food and drink strengthen us
in our new life in Christ,
who is Lord forever and ever. Amen.

T HE LORD LIVES!
Blessed be our rock,
and exalted be the God of our salvation
who delivered his son from death
by raising him to new life.
May our Easter meal be a hymn of praise
to the One who is Father, Son, and Holy Spirit
forever and ever. Amen.

O Lord,
   you have granted our hearts' desire
by raising Jesus from the dead.
Through your Holy Spirit,
fulfill all your plans in us.
May we shout for joy over your victory
and in your name lift up banners of praise.
Bless this Easter food and drink
as we take pride in your name,
Father, Son, and Holy Spirit,
One God, forever and ever. Amen.

O LORD, OUR SHEPHERD,
   you have brought us
to the green pastures of your grace
and the still waters of our baptismal death
and resurrection into Christ.
Continue to lead us in right paths,
even when we walk through the darkest valleys of fear.
You have prepared this Easter table before us.
Through your blessing on us and this food,
grant us your goodness and mercy
all the days of our lives.
May we dwell in your presence with your Son
and your Holy Spirit forever and ever. Amen.

O LORD,
    you are our light and our salvation.
You are the stronghold of our lives.
The brightness of the resurrection of Christ
has shattered the darkness of our world
and made our faces glow with the new life
he has bestowed through the Holy Spirit.
As we share these Easter gifts of food and drink,
grant that we may dwell in your presence
all the days of our lives
and one day behold your beauty in heaven,
where you live and reign as one God,
forever and ever. Amen.

G LORY TO YOU, O LORD.
Your powerful voice has thundered
over the waters of baptism
and claimed us as your adopted children.
Your mighty voice has flashed flames of fire
through the Holy Spirit,
who has made us priests, prophets,
and kings in your sight.
Your great voice has raised the broken body of Jesus
from the dead and given it to us in Eucharist.
For these Easter sacraments
we never cease to praise you.
Through this food and drink,
bless us and strengthen us.
We ask this through Christ our Lord. Amen.

O LORD,
you turn mourning into dancing
and remove our Lenten sackcloth of repentance
with the resurrection of Jesus from the dead.
Our souls praise you
and our lives proclaim your goodness.
Bless our food and drink
that we may give you thanks forever
through Christ our Lord. Amen.

YOUR STEADFAST LOVE, O LORD,
extends to the heavens.
Your faithfulness stretches to the clouds.
Your righteousness is like the mighty mountains.
Your judgments are like the great deep.
Through the resurrection of your son,
you have saved humans and animals alike.
We declare your steadfast love
as we feast on this abundance.
All glory to you, Father, Son, and Holy Spirit,
one God forever and ever. Amen.

O Lord,
 you are the salvation of the righteous;
you are our refuge in times of trouble.
You rescued your son from the snares of death
by opening his tomb and raising him to new life.
Come to our aid and rescue us,
for we take refuge in you.
Bless this food we share in honor
of the resurrection of Jesus Christ,
who is Lord forever and ever. Amen.

B E EXALTED, O GOD, ABOVE THE HEAVENS.
 Let your glory be over all the earth.
Through the resurrection of Christ from death
you have awakened the dawn with song.
Keep our hearts steadfast
as we sing and feast this Easter season.
We ask this through Christ our Lord. Amen.

WE GIVE THANKS TO YOU, O LORD,
among the peoples.
We give thanks to you for your gifts of food and drink.
We sing your praises here at our table.
Through the resurrection of your son,
you have shown your steadfast love
and your faithfulness.
Be exalted above the heavens, O God.
Let your glory be over all the earth forever and ever.
Amen.

WE SING OF YOUR MIGHT, O LORD GOD.
We sing aloud of your steadfast love.
Through your strength,
you have raised your son from death to life.
We praise you for this Easter food and drink.
Receive our thanksgiving through Christ our Lord.
Amen.

ALL PRAISE IS DUE TO YOU, O GOD,
for you have answered the prayer of your son
and raised him from the dead to glory in your sight.
As we celebrate his resurrection and await our own,
bless this Easter food and drink
that it may satisfy us with your goodness.
Hear our prayer through Christ our Lord.
Amen.

O GOD OF OUR SALVATION,
by your strength you established the mountains.
You silence the roaring of the waves of the seas.
We who live at earth's farthest bounds are awed
by the signs of your awesome deeds.
We stand in awe of your Easter light
and the new life you granted to your son
through his resurrection from the dead.
Through your blessing upon our food,
grant us a share in his glory,
so that morning and evening
we may shout praise to you.
We ask this through Christ our Lord. Amen.

WE MAKE A JOYFUL NOISE TO YOU, O GOD.
We sing the glory of your name
this Easter season.
We give you glorious praise
for the resurrection of Christ.
Indeed, how awesome are your deeds!
Bless our food and drink.
May we join with all the earth in worshiping you
and singing praises to your name
through Christ our Lord. Amen.

WE COME TO SEE WHAT YOU HAVE DONE, O GOD,
to marvel at your deeds among mortals.
You turned the waves of the baptismal sea
into the dry land of new life.
And so we rejoice in you for our baptism in Christ.
May this meal help us celebrate our Easter faith
so that your praises may be heard throughout the earth.
We ask this through Christ our Lord. Amen.

B LESSED ARE YOU, O LORD,
for daily you bear us up.
You are the God of our salvation.
You are the God who enabled his son
to escape from death and rise to eternal life.
As you have shown your might, O God,
show your strength to us
and bless this food and drink.
Grant that we may share in the new life
won for us through Jesus Christ our Lord. Amen.

E TERNAL GOD,
during this Easter season,
we call to mind your deeds
and remember your wonders of old.
We meditate on the resurrection of your son
and muse on your holiness.
As we celebrate with this food and drink,
make us grow in your ways.
Work great wonders among us
through Jesus Christ our Lord. Amen.

O SHEPHERD OF ISRAEL,
 you hear our cries and you come to save us.
Restore us, O God, like you restored your son,
and let your face shine upon us that we may be saved.
May this food and drink that we share
in honor of Christ's resurrection
strengthen us in your service.
Hear us through the same Christ our Lord. Amen.

O LORD, IN YOU STEADFAST LOVE
 and faithfulness meet,
righteousness and peace kiss each other.
Through the resurrection of your son,
faithfulness has sprung up from the ground
and righteousness looks down from the sky.
You give us what is good
and our land has yielded its increase.
Bless this food that we use
to celebrate the resurrection of Christ,
and guide us in the steps of him
who is Lord forever and ever. Amen.

O LORD, YOU ARE KING.
The earth rejoices in you.
Even the coastlands are glad
in the resurrection of your Son.
The clouds and thick darkness of night
have given way to the bright sun of this Easter day.
Hear our praise and bless our food and drink,
O Lord of all the earth, forever and ever. Amen.

O LORD, YOU ARE MOST HIGH OVER ALL THE EARTH.
You are exalted above the heavens.
To your glory you raised your son, Jesus Christ,
from the sleep of death.
May the heavens proclaim your righteousness
as we behold your Easter glory.
Guard our lives and strengthen our faith
as we eat this food you set before us.
We rejoice in you, O Lord,
and we give thanks to your holy name
now and forever. Amen.

W E MAKE A JOYFUL NOISE TO YOU, O LORD,
breaking into joyous song and singing praises.
The seas roar; the waters clap their hands;
the hills sing together for joy
at the thought of your resurrected son.
He judges the world with righteousness.
May this Easter food and drink strengthen us
to praise you now and forever. Amen.

M IGHTY KING, LOVER OF JUSTICE, YOU ARE LORD.
All people tremble before you;
even the earth quakes.
We praise your great and awesome name.
Holy are you!
We extol you, our God, for the resurrection of Christ,
even as we ask your blessing upon this food and drink.
We worship before you.
Holy are you forever and ever. Amen.

YOU ARE EXALTED ABOVE THE HEAVENS, O GOD,
and your glory shines over all the earth.
Your steadfast love is manifest
in the resurrection of Christ.
We praise you for the new life
you give to us in the waters of baptism.
Raise your hand in blessing over our food
that we may be strengthened to do your will
through the same Jesus Christ our Lord. Amen.

O LORD, OUR STRENGTH AND OUR MIGHT,
you have brought salvation to the earth
through the death and resurrection of Jesus Christ.
You have exalted him at your right hand.
Through the waters of baptism,
you have raised us to new life with him.
May this Easter food and drink
help his new life to surge within us.
We ask this through the same Christ our Lord. Amen.

LORD JESUS CHRIST,
you took the form of a servant
and were born in human likeness.
Through the humility of your cross,
you have redeemed the world.
As we celebrate your exaltation at God's right hand,
bless this food and drink we share.
We praise your name forever and ever. Amen.

ALMIGHTY GOD,
you have decreed that at Jesus' name
every knee must bend in the heavens,
on the earth, and under the earth.
Bless this Easter food and drink
which we use to celebrate Christ's resurrection.
May our tongues proclaim your glory forever and ever.
Amen.

O GOD, YOU HAVE DEMONSTRATED YOUR POWER
by raising your son from death to life.
Through his resurrection,
you have wedded heaven to earth.
As we celebrate this wedding feast of the Lamb,
bless all who share our food and drink.
All praise be yours forever and ever. Amen.

B LESSED MAY YOU BE, O LORD, OUR GOD,
from eternity to eternity.
Yours are grandeur and power,
majesty, splendor, and glory.
Bless this food that comes from your hands,
as we give you thanks for the resurrection of your son
and praise the majesty of your name forever and ever.
Amen.

PRAISE BE TO YOU, GOD AND FATHER
of our Lord Jesus Christ.
You have bestowed on us in Christ
every spiritual blessing.
Through the waters of baptism,
you make us holy and blameless in your sight.
Send your blessing upon all gathered at this table.
Grant that we may never cease
to praise you now and forever. Amen.

O LORD, THROUGH YOUR SON, JESUS CHRIST,
you have predestined us
to be your adopted children.
We praise your glorious favor of redemption
through his cross and resurrection.
May this food and drink give us the wisdom
to understand fully the mystery of your plan
that you will bring all things into one in him,
who is Lord forever and ever. Amen.

W E BLESS YOU, O GOD, FOR YOU LIVE FOREVER.
We exalt you before every living being
for the resurrection of your son.
Also, for this food and drink we praise you.
We bless you and exalt you name forever and ever.
Amen.

O LORD, YOU HAVE MADE YOUR SON
the head of the body, the church.
He who is the beginning,
the firstborn of the dead,
made peace through the blood of his cross.
May our celebration of his resurrection
bring peace to all who share this food and drink.
Hear us through Christ our Lord. Amen.

Salvation and power have come, O Lord,
through the resurrection
of your Anointed One, Jesus Christ.
May the blood of the Lamb cleanse us of our sins
and enable us to celebrate this Easter feast with joy.
We ask this through the same Jesus Christ,
who lives and reigns with you and the Holy Spirit,
one God, forever and ever. Amen.

O Lord, you are the creator of the heavens
and the designer of the earth.
In the fullness of time,
you revealed yourself in the person of your son.
Through his death and resurrection,
he has redeemed us.
May this food and drink enable us
to follow him faithfully,
for he lives and reigns with you forever and ever.
Amen.

L ORD GOD, MIGHTY AND WONDERFUL ARE YOUR WORKS.
Righteous and true are your ways.
We honor your name and give you glory
for raising Jesus Christ from death to life.
Make holy this food before us,
and accept our praise in your presence.
We ask this through the same Jesus Christ our Lord.
Amen.

W E PRAISE YOU, O LORD,
for you are gloriously triumphant.
When your son slept in death,
you awakened him with the breath of the Holy Spirit.
You are our strength and our courage,
and we praise you for this Easter day.
Bless this food and those gathered here to share it.
We praise you through Jesus Christ our Lord. Amen.

B LESSED ARE YOU, O LORD,
praiseworthy and exalted above all forever.
Blessed is your holy and glorious name,
praiseworthy and exalted above all forever.
We bless you for this Easter food and drink.
As we celebrate the resurrection of Christ, your son,
make us truly grateful for all your works.
May you be praised now and forever. Amen.

H OLY ONE, OUR LORD AND GOD,
you make us confident and unafraid
as we celebrate the resurrection of Christ.
Grant that this food may give us strength and courage
to pick up our crosses and follow him
through death to new life.
We give you praise for all your deeds
and we exalt your name forever and ever. Amen.

O LORD GOD,
through the death and resurrection of your son,
you have sprinkled clean water upon us
and cleansed us of all impurities.
We give you thanks for the new heart
and the new spirit you have placed within us.
Strengthen us through this food and drink
that we may live by your commandments.
We ask this through Christ our Lord. Amen.

Ascension

WE SING PRAISE TO YOU, O LORD.
We sing praise to you, our King.
With the sound of the trumpet
you have raised your son from death
and seated him at your right hand in glory.
May our celebration of his ascension
and this food and drink we share
be acceptable praise and thanks in your presence.
You are King of all the earth, O Lord,
forever and ever. Amen.

Pentecost

O LORD, CREATOR OF ALL THAT EXISTS.
When you take away your spirit, all things die.
When you send forth you spirit, all things come to life
and you renew the face of the earth.
Send your Holy Spirit to breathe new life into us
through our sharing of this Pentecost food and drink.
May your glory, Lord, endure forever.
May you always rejoice in your works
through Jesus Christ our Lord. Amen.

WE GIVE THANKS TO YOUR NAME, O LORD,
for through the death
and resurrection of your son,
you have established a new and lasting Jerusalem.
Grant peace within the walls of this home
and grant that this Pentecost food and drink
will enable us to preserve that peace
through Jesus Christ our Lord. Amen.

O LORD, HOW WONDERFUL ARE ALL THE WORKS
OF YOUR HAND.

Long ago you formed us in our mothers' wombs;
you knitted us together in secret
when only you could see our unformed substance.
Search us and know our hearts.
Send the spirit of Pentecost
to bring us into your presence
and refashion us in the image of your son.
Bless this food that adds life to our days with you.
All praise to you, Father, Son, and Holy Spirit,
one God living and reigning forever and ever. Amen.

The Season
of Ordinary Time

L ORD,
the trees planted beside flowing streams
have yielded their fruit.
Bless this food we are about to eat,
that it may make us prosper in your sight.
We ask this through Christ our Lord. Amen.

O LORD,
you watch over the way of the righteous.
Grant that we may be planted
by the streams of your grace
and be made worthy of your blessing upon our food.
Hear us through Christ our Lord. Amen.

O LORD, YOU ARE A SHIELD AROUND US.
When we cry to you, you answer us.
Bless this food and keep us safe.
We ask this through Christ our Lord. Amen.

S USTAINING LORD,
we lie down and sleep and awaken and get up
and you keep watch over us.
Keep us safe as we eat and drink in your sight.
We give you thanks for this food
through Jesus Christ our Lord. Amen.

R ISE UP, O LORD!
Deliver us from the foolishness of our ways.
Grant your blessing upon all gathered here
and on the food that comes from your hand.
We praise you through Christ our Lord. Amen.

O UR KING AND OUR GOD,
listen to the sound of our prayer.
In the morning you hear our voices.
In the evening you rain your blessings
upon the food that we are about to share.
We bow down in gratitude to you
through Jesus Christ our Lord. Amen.

O LORD, THOSE WHO ABIDE WITH YOU
walk blamelessly and do what is right,
speaking the truth from their hearts.
Grant your blessing upon this food,
that it may strengthen us
to be found righteous in your sight.
We ask this through Christ our Lord. Amen.

O LORD, YOU ARE OUR ROCK AND FORTRESS;
you lead us and guide us.
Do not let us be trapped in the net of empty promises;
do not let us be snared by passing pleasures.
Stretch out your hand in blessing on our food
as we commit our spirits into your hands.
You have redeemed us, faithful God,
through the death and resurrection of Jesus Christ,
who is Lord forever and ever. Amen.

Your light and your truth lead us, O Lord.
They bring us to your holy church, your dwelling.
We go to your altar with joy
and we praise you with song.
Bless this food you give us.
May it be our help and strength.
Hear us through Christ our Lord. Amen.

O God, we have heard with our ears
what deeds you performed in the past.
In the fullness of time,
you brought to birth your son,
who, through his death and resurrection,
has brought us the fullness of redemption.
May our food and drink remind us
to boast continually of you
and give thanks to you forever and ever. Amen.

O UR KING AND OUR GOD,
   you know the secrets of our hearts.
Rise up, come to our help.
Redeem us for the sake of your steadfast love.
We lift up our hands in thanksgiving to you
for this food and drink.
Bless it through Christ our Lord. Amen.

W E ARE LIKE GREEN OLIVE TREES
   in your house, O God.
We trust in your steadfast love.
We thank you for all you have done for us
and for this food and drink that you set before us.
We will proclaim you name
in the presence of all the faithful forever
through Jesus Christ our Lord. Amen.

F ROM THE HEAVENS YOU LOOK UPON US, O LORD.
You seek the wise who walk in your ways.
Bless this food and drink we set before you.
Grant that it may impart wisdom to us
and bring us to your kingdom
where you live with your son, Jesus Christ,
and the Holy Spirit, one God, forever and ever. Amen.

M IGHTY GOD, THE EARTH HAS YIELDED ITS INCREASE,
and we feast with delight
at what you have given to us.
Raise your hand in blessing over this food
and all who gather around this table to share it,
through Jesus Christ our Lord. Amen.

W E SING TO YOU, O GOD,
we sing praises to your name.
You have sent the rain to grow our food
and harvesters to gather it.
As we prepare to share this meal,
make us overflow with thanksgiving.
May we be exultant before you
and praise you always through Christ our Lord. Amen.

O UR PRAYER IS TO YOU, O LORD.
At an acceptable time
and in the abundance of your steadfast love,
answer us, O God.
Do not hide your face,
but bless this food and drink
that we have set before you.
Hear our prayer through Christ our Lord. Amen.

O UR MOUTHS TELL OF YOUR RIGHTEOUS ACTS, O GOD.
We praise your mighty deeds of salvation.
Though their number is past our knowledge,
we come praising you for this food and drink.
Bless it and use it to strengthen us in your service.
We ask this through Christ our Lord. Amen.

T RULY, YOU ARE GOOD TO US, O GOD.
Our feet have almost stumbled;
our steps have nearly slipped into sin.
But you keep our hearts clean
and wash our hands in innocence.
Grant that this food will strengthen us
in our resolve to be pleasing in your sight,
O Lord, our Rock and our Redeemer, forever and ever.
Amen.

Most High God,
you are our rock and our redeemer.
You lead your people like sheep
and guide them like a flock.
Bring us into the safety of your presence.
May your blessing be upon our meal
and upon our sharing around this table.
We give thanks to you
through Jesus Christ our Lord forever and ever. Amen.

We come before you, O Lord,
making a joyful noise.
We come before you, O Lord,
worshiping you with gladness.
We come into your presence with singing.
We know that you are God over all the earth.
You made us, and we are yours.
Sustain us with your blessing upon this food
as we give thanks to you and bless your name
forever and ever. Amen.

O LORD OUR GOD,
long ago you laid the foundations of the earth;
the heavens are the work of your hands.
All things will perish, but you endure.
All things wear out and pass away,
but you are the same, and you have no end.
Make us grateful for the years of our lives
and strengthen us through your blessing
upon this food.
Hear our prayer through Christ our Lord. Amen.

WE BLESS YOU O LORD.
All that is within us blesses your holy name.
You forgive our iniquity, heal our diseases,
redeem our lives, and crown us
with your steadfast love and mercy.
Grant that this food and drink
will bring satisfaction to our lives
and renew our strength and courage.
We pray through Christ our Lord. Amen.

L ORD, YOU RULE OVER ALL
from your throne in the heavens.
Bless the Lord, O you his angels.
Bless the Lord, all you his ministers.
Bless the Lord, all you his works.
Bless the Lord, all you gathered here
for his steadfast love and everlasting mercy
in providing us with food and drink.
We bless the Lord through his son, Jesus Christ. Amen.

W E BLESS THE LORD, THE GREAT GOD
of all the world.
He is clothed with honor and majesty,
wrapped in light as with a garment.
He stretches out the heavens like a tent,
setting the beams of his chambers on the waters.
He makes the clouds his chariot,
ridding on the wings of the wind.
We bless the Lord, the great God of all the world
for this food and drink which he sets before us.
We bless him through Christ our Lord. Amen.

O LORD, HOW MANIFOLD ARE YOUR WORKS.
In your wisdom you have made all things
and filled the earth with your creatures.
All look to you to give them food in due season.
When you give it to them, they gather it up;
when you open your hand,
all are filled with good things.
We bless you for all that you have set on our table.
May we never cease to praise you
through Christ our Lord. Amen.

WE GIVE THANKS TO YOU, O LORD,
and we call upon your name
as we make known your deeds among all people.
We sing praise to you
for all your wonderful works,
especially for this food and drink.
We give glory to your name,
Father, Son, and Holy Spirit,
one God forever and ever. Amen.

PRAISE BE TO YOU, O LORD.
We give thanks to you, for you are good.
Your steadfast love endures forever.
Remember us in your mercy
and bless the food and drink we are about to share.
All good things come from your hand
through Jesus Christ our Lord. Amen.

O LORD OF STEADFAST LOVE,
you show wonderful works to humankind.
You satisfy the thirsty
and fill the hungry with good things.
Bless our drink and food
and lead us to your kingdom
where you live and reign
as Father, Son, and Holy Spirit,
one God, forever and ever. Amen.

W<small>E THANK YOU, O L</small>ORD, <small>FOR YOUR STEADFAST LOVE</small>
and we offer ourselves
as a thanksgiving sacrifice to you.
Sustain us with your Holy Spirit
and bless this food which comes from your hand.
Hear us through Christ our Lord. Amen.

O <small>L</small>ORD, <small>GIVER OF ALL GOOD GIFTS,</small>
others have sown the fields
and planted the crops,
but we are the beneficiaries of their fruitful yield.
As you blessed the work of their hands,
so bless this food and drink
and all gathered around this table.
We ask this through Christ our Lord. Amen.

OUR HEARTS ARE STEADFAST, O GOD.
We sing and make melody to you
at morning, noon, and night,
giving thanks to you, O Lord.
Your steadfast love is higher than the heavens,
and your faithfulness reaches to the clouds.
Make us even more grateful for this food and drink.
Hear our prayer through Christ our Lord. Amen.

WE GIVE THANKS TO YOU, O LORD,
with all our hearts.
Great are your works, O Lord, studied
by all who delight in them.
You provide food and drink for those who fear you;
ever mindful of your covenant,
we give you thanks for what you have set on our table.
Through the death and resurrection of Christ,
you have redeemed us and established
an everlasting covenant.
Holy and awesome is your name forever and ever.
Amen.

THE PRAISE OF YOUR NAME ENDURES FOREVER, O LORD.
Happy are those who fear you
and delight in your commands.
Make us gracious, merciful, and righteous
through our sharing of this food and drink.
Keep our hearts steady
that one day we may be exalted in honor before you,
Father, Son, and Holy Spirit, one God,
forever and ever. Amen.

BLESSED IS YOUR NAME, O LORD,
from this time on and forevermore.
From the rising of the sun to its setting,
your name is to be praised.
From your dwelling above the heavens
you shower us with these blessings of food and drink.
May all your gifts strengthen us, your servants,
and lead us to the peace of your kingdom
where you live forever and ever. Amen.

Not to ourselves, O Lord, not to ourselves,
but to you do we give glory
for the sake of your steadfast love and faithfulness.
You bless this house with these gifts of food and drink.
Accept the thanks of all gathered here,
maker of heaven and earth.
We praise you forever through Christ our Lord. Amen.

O Lord, you are righteous and merciful.
We rest secure in the bounty from your hand
for which we cannot return payment.
Hear our thanksgiving prayers of sacrifice
as we call upon your name through Christ our Lord.
Amen.

Let your steadfast love come to us, O Lord,
your salvation according to your promise.
We trust in your word of blessing
that this food and drink will sustain us in your service.
We pray through Christ our Lord. Amen.

O LORD, YOUR WORD GIVES US HOPE,
and your promise gives us life.
As we remember your name,
bless this food and drink
which come from the bounty of your hand.
Hear our prayer through Christ our Lord. Amen.

YOU DEAL WELL WITH US, YOUR SERVANTS, O LORD,
according to your word.
Teach us good judgment and knowledge.
May this food enable us to pursue your wisdom
all the days of our lives.
We ask this through Christ our Lord. Amen.

YOU EXIST FOREVER, O LORD,
and your word is firmly fixed in heaven.
Your faithfulness endures to all generations.
As all things serve you,
grant that we may be counted among your servants.
May this food and drink strengthen us
through Jesus Christ, your son, our Lord. Amen.

O LORD, YOUR WORD IS SWEET TO OUR TASTE;
it is sweeter than honey to our mouths.
Your word is a lamp to our feet
and a light to our path.
Accept our offerings of praise
and speak your word of blessing on this meal.
Hear our prayer through Jesus Christ our Lord. Amen.

THE UNFOLDING OF YOUR WORDS, O LORD, GIVES LIGHT;
it imparts understanding to the simple.
Turn to us and be gracious to us;
plant your words deep into our hearts.
Strengthened by your blessing
upon this food and drink,
help us to keep our steps steady
according to your promise.
You are God forever and ever. Amen.

O LORD, YOU BLESS US WITH LIFE
and feed us with food from your hand.
May all who share this meal
live together in unity and peace.
We ask this through Christ our Lord. Amen.

WE, YOUR SERVANTS, COME BEFORE YOU, O LORD,
and we bless your holy name.
You are the maker of heaven and earth,
and you share with us all good things.
Make us grateful for this food and drink;
bless all gathered at this table.
Hear us through Christ our Lord. Amen.

WE PRAISE YOU, O LORD.
All your servants praise your name, O Lord.
You are good and gracious.
Your greatness is acclaimed in heaven and on earth.
Shower your blessings upon this meal
that we are about to share.
May your name endure forever,
and your renown throughout all ages
forever and ever. Amen.

WE GIVE THANKS TO YOU, O LORD,
for you are good
and your steadfast love endures forever.
Remember us, your servants,
who gather to share this food and drink.
We give thanks to you, O Lord,
for your steadfast love endures forever. Amen.

O LORD, YOU TEACH US TO DO YOUR WILL
　　for you are our God.
Let your good spirit lead us on a level path.
Preserve our lives through this food and drink
for we hunger and thirst for you.
Accept our prayer through Christ our Lord. Amen.

WE EXTOL YOU, OUR GOD AND KING,
　　and we bless your name forever and ever.
Great are you, O Lord, and greatly to be praised
for this meal which you have given to us.
Even though your greatness is unsearchable,
we proclaim aloud your mercy and steadfast love.
Hear our prayer through Christ our Lord. Amen.

O LORD, YOU ARE GRACIOUS AND MERCIFUL,
abounding in steadfast love.
You are good to all,
and compassionate to everything you have made.
All your works give you thanks
and we, your faithful people, bless you.
This food and drink speak of your power
and make known to us your mighty deeds.
May your kingdom endure through every generation,
Father, Son, and Holy Spirit,
one God, forever and ever. Amen.

F AITHFUL AND GRACIOUS GOD,
the eyes of all people look to you,
and you give them their food in due season.
You open your hand
and satisfy the desire of every living thing.
Our mouths speak your praise
for this food and drink,
and we bless your holy name forever and ever. Amen.

I T IS GOOD THAT WE PRAISE YOUR NAME, O LORD.
It is fitting that we thank you for the rain
that waters the earth and brings forth food.
Bless this meal which comes from your bounty,
and bless all who sit at this table.
May we praise you forever and ever. Amen.

W E PRAISE YOUR NAME, O LORD.
We praise you for the sun
and the moon and the stars.
We praise you for the snow and the sleet and the rain.
We praise you for the mountains and the hills,
for the fruit trees and the cedars,
for cattle, pigs, and chickens.
From your creation you feed us,
and we praise your exalted name forever and ever.
Amen.

O LORD, YOU TAKE PLEASURE IN YOUR PEOPLE;
the faithful exult in your glory.
Accept the thanksgiving we offer to you
for this food and drink which you set before us.
Hear us through Christ our Lord. Amen.

O LORD OF MERCY,
you made all things by your word
spoken through the wisdom of the Holy Spirit.
Send forth your wisdom
that it may be with us and work in us
and tell us what is pleasing to you.
Help us to gain wisdom
through our sharing of this food.
Grant what we ask through Christ our Lord. Amen.

Solemnities
and Feasts

Solemnity of Mary, Mother of God
January 1

You have multiplied your wondrous deeds,
through the birth of your son, O Lord.
No one can compare to him, born of the Virgin Mary.
Through your blessing upon our food and drink,
enable us to proclaim your deeds throughout the world.
We ask this through our Lord Jesus Christ, your son,
who lives and reigns with you and the Holy Spirit,
one God forever and ever. Amen.

Solemnity of the Epiphany of the Lord
Sunday between January 2 and 8

Blessed are you, O Lord, our God,
for your glory fills the whole earth.
Through your holy light,
you have revealed your son to all the nations.
May his name endure forever.
May all the nations be blessed by him.
As we celebrate this feast of his Epiphany,
graciously bless our food and drink
that all gathered at this table may serve you in love.
Blessed be your glorious name forever and ever. Amen.

Feast of the Baptism of the Lord
Sunday after Epiphany

O GOD, WHEN THE WATERS SAW YOU,
they were afraid and trembled.
As Jesus entered the Jordan River,
your voice thundered from the sky
and your light lit up the world.
You led your son
through the river of death of resurrection,
yet your footprints were unseen.
Grant that this food may strengthen us
so that we may live our baptism
into his cross and new life.
He lives and reigns with you and the Holy Spirit,
one God forever and ever. Amen.

Feast of the Presentation of the Lord
February 2

O LORD, WE HAVE SOUGHT YOU,
and you answered us
and delivered us from all our fears.
As we celebrate the feast of the presentation
of your son,
we come ready to listen to your word.
Look upon us and our food
and raise your hand of blessing toward us.
May we walk always in your ways of peace.
We ask this through Christ our Lord. Amen.

Feast of the Chair of St. Peter
February 22

W E PROCLAIM YOUR STEADFAST LOVE,
O Lord, forever.
With our mouths we announce your faithfulness
to all generations.
Your son established your Church
upon the rock of Peter's faith
and you have kept your covenant to remain with us
until the end of time.
As we celebrate the feast of the Chair of St. Peter,
we praise your love and faithfulness
for the past millennia.
Bless this food and drink we share
and keep us enfolded in your Church
until Christ returns in glory.
We ask this through the same Christ our Lord. Amen.

Solemnity of Joseph, Husband of Mary
March 19

T HE RIGHTEOUS REJOICE IN YOU, O LORD,
because you fill the earth with your steadfast love.
We praise you with loud shouts
as we celebrate the feast of St. Joseph,
husband of Mary and foster-father of Jesus.
Bless this food and all gathered at this table.
May our sharing here
strengthen us with your righteousness and justice.
We ask this through Christ our Lord.Amen.

Solemnity of the Annunciation
March 25

B Y YOUR WORD, O LORD, THE HEAVENS WERE MADE.
By your word, your son took flesh
in the womb of the Blessed Virgin Mary.
We stand in awe of you
for you spoke, and all came to be.
Speak your blessing upon our food
that we may be strengthened to hear your word
and bring your good tidings to all we meet.
We ask this through Christ our Lord. Amen.

Feast of St. Mark
April 25

O GOD, YOU ARE OUR GOD; WE SEEK YOU.
Our souls thirst for you;
our flesh faints for you.
We have beheld your power and glory
in the words of the gospel of your son.
On this feast of St. Mark we praise you
and give you thanks for this food and drink.
We will bless you as long as we live
lifting up our hands and calling on your name
through Jesus Christ our Lord. Amen.

Feast of Sts. Philip and James
May 3

OUR SOULS ARE SATISFIED AS WITH A RICH FEAST
and our mouths praise you
with joyful lips, O God.
We think of you throughout the day
and we meditate on you throughout the night.
You are our help
and in the shadow of your wings we shout for joy
as we ask your blessing upon this food.
Like your apostles Philip and James,
may we never cease to announce
the good news of your son,
who lives and reigns with you and the Holy Spirit,
one God forever and ever. Amen.

Feast of St. Matthias
May 14

How great are your works, O Lord.
Your thoughts are very deep.
The dullard cannot know
and the stupid cannot understand your ways.
As we celebrate the feast of St. Matthias,
grant that through the intercession of your apostle,
we may grow in grace through this food
and drink we share.
Hear our prayer through Christ our Lord. Amen.

Feast of the Visitation
May 31

L ET THE HEAVENS PRAISE YOUR WONDERS, O LORD.
Let your people praise your faithfulness.
No one is as mighty as you.
As we celebrate the visit of Mary to Elizabeth,
we remember your loving kindness to us
through this food and drink.
Bless these gifts and bless us
as you blessed Mary and Elizabeth.
All thanks to you, Father, Son, and Holy Spirit,
God forever and ever. Amen.

SOLEMNITY OF THE HOLY TRINITY
SUNDAY AFTER PENTECOST

O Lord, God of all,
the heavens are yours, the earth is yours,
the world and all that is in it belongs to you.
You created the north and the south,
the east and the west.
In your steadfast love and faithfulness
you have revealed the mystery of your inner being:
one God, three persons.
As we celebrate this feast in your triune honor,
bless all who share this food and drink.
May we never cease to praise you for your bounty.
You are Father, Son, and Holy Spirit,
one God, living and reigning forever and ever. Amen.

Solemnity of the Body and Blood of Christ
Second Sunday after Pentecost

W E BLESS YOU, LORD, AT ALL TIMES.
Words of praise are continually in our mouths.
We magnify you and exalt your name.
On this feast of the Body and Blood of your son
we taste and see how good you are
as we prepare to share this food and drink.
May your gifts make us hunger ever more
for the bread of life, Jesus Christ,
who is Lord forever and ever. Amen.

Solemnity of the Sacred Heart
Friday after Second Sunday after Pentecost

W E DELIGHT TO DO YOUR WILL, O LORD;
your law is written within our hearts.
We proclaim your faithfulness and salvation;
we announce your steadfast love.
Bless this food we share
and continue to pour on us your mercy
that will keep us safe forever
through Jesus Christ our Lord. Amen.

Solemnity of the Birth of John the Baptist
June 24

As the deer longs for flowing streams,
so our souls long for you, O God.
We thirst for you, the living God,
and you give us to drink of living water.
As we celebrate the birth of John the Baptist
with this food and drink,
renew in us the river of our baptism.
Blessed may you be, Lord God,
from everlasting to everlasting. Amen.

Solemnity of Sts. Peter and Paul
June 29

You look down from the heavens, O Lord,
and you see all humankind.
From your throne you watch
all the inhabitants of the earth.
As we celebrate the feast of your apostles,
Peter and Paul,
we ask that you bless this table and its food
and that you fashion our hearts like you did theirs.
We ask this through Christ our Lord. Amen.

Feast of St. Thomas
July 3

O LORD, GOD OF ALL,
righteousness and justice are the foundation
of your throne;
steadfast love and faithfulness go before you.
Happy are the people who exult in your name.
On this feast of your apostle Thomas,
we ask that you grant us your strength
in times of doubt
that we may proclaim the name
of your son, Jesus Christ,
with fitting honor and praise.
This food and drink come from your bounty
and so we praise you for your gifts, O Holy One,
through Christ our Lord. Amen.

Feast of St. James
July 25

WE GIVE THANKS TO YOU, O LORD;
we sing praises to your name, O Most High,
as we celebrate the feast of your apostle James.
We declare your steadfast love in the morning
and your faithfulness throughout the night.
O Lord, you have made us glad by your work
and we ask your blessing upon this meal
we are about to share.
We praise you with joy through Christ our Lord.
Amen.

Feast of the Transfiguration
August 6

O God, you are more majestic
than the everlasting mountains.
No one can stand in your light
without being transformed by your presence.
May this food and drink serve
to configure us more and more
into the image of your son, Jesus Christ,
who is Lord forever and ever. Amen.

FEAST OF ST. LAWRENCE
AUGUST 10

Those who love you, Most High God, you deliver.

You protect those who know your name.

When they call, you answer them.

You are with them in trouble.

You rescue them and honor them.

As we celebrate this feast

of the martyrdom of St. Lawrence,

grant us a long life in your presence.

Bless this food and drink

and show us your salvation through Christ our Lord.

Amen.

Solemnity of the Assumption
August 15

We sing to you, O God;
we sing praise to your name.
From the sleep of death you awakened
the mother of your son
and let her share in the eternal life
he won through his own death and resurrection.
She heard your mighty voice and answered your call.
Awesome are you, O God,
as you bless us with this food and drink.
Raise us to share the glory of the Virgin Mary.
Blessed are you, Father, Son, and Holy Spirit,
one God forever and ever. Amen.

Feast of St. Bartholomew
August 24

MAY HEAVEN AND EARTH PRAISE YOU, O GOD;
may the seas and everything
that moves in them
sing praise to your name, O Most High.
Through your apostle Bartholomew,
you have spread the good news of your son
and called your people to return to you.
May this food and drink strengthen us
to follow in the footsteps of Jesus Christ,
who is Lord forever and ever. Amen.

Feast of the Birth of Mary
September 8

W E PRAISE YOUR NAME WITH A SONG, O GOD.
We magnify you with thanksgiving
as we celebrate the feast of the birth of the Virgin Mary.
Shower your blessings upon our food and drink
and grant that we may be found acceptable
in your sight.
We ask this through our Lord Jesus Christ, your son,
who lives and reigns with you and the Holy Spirit,
one God forever and ever. Amen.

Feast of the Triumph of the Cross
September 14

Y OUR THRONE, O GOD, ENDURES FOREVER.
Your royal scepter is the cross of your son,
whom you anointed with the oil of gladness.
May we love your righteousness and justice.
May this food and drink bring grace to our lips.
Be pleased with our theme of thanks, O Lord,
through Jesus Christ your son,
whose cross has redeemed the world forever and ever.
Amen.

Feast of St. Matthew
September 21

MOST HIGH GOD, WE LIVE IN YOUR SHELTER;
we abide in your shadow, Almighty One.
You deliver us from the evil of the day and night.
You instruct us through the gospel of your son.
As we celebrate this feast of St. Matthew,
bless our food and drink
and grant that no evil befall us
because we have made you our refuge
and dwelling place.
Hear us through Christ our Lord. Amen.

Feast of Sts. Michael, Gabriel, and Raphael
September 29

O GOD, YOU VISIT THE EARTH AND WATER IT;
you greatly enrich it with showers.
You provide us with grain and bless its growth.
You send your holy angels as messengers
to announce your mighty deeds.
May we hear their good news
as we eat this meal in joy
and praise you forever through Christ our Lord. Amen.

Feast of St. Luke
October 18

A LL THE PEOPLES PRAISE YOU, O GOD,
for the words of your evangelist Luke.
May this food and drink
serve to strengthen us to be messengers of his gospel,
which announces the good news of your son,
Jesus Christ, who is Lord forever and ever. Amen.

Feast of Sts. Simon and Jude
October 28

O LORD, WE PRAISE YOUR NAME.
The righteous flourish like a palm tree
and grow like a cedar in your sight.
Planted in your presence they flourish.
As we celebrate the feast
of your apostles Simon and Jude,
grant your blessing upon our food
that we may flourish in your sight.
You are our rock and our redeemer,
O Lord, forever and ever. Amen.

Solemnity of All Saints
November 1

O Lord, you have given us days in your service,
but in your sight a lifetime is as nothing.
Like your faithful saints of the past,
all our hope is placed in you.
Hear our prayer, O Lord,
as we share this food on the festival of your saints.
Through it bless our lives,
which are like passing guests on the earth,
and bring us to the eternal life you promise
through Jesus Christ our Lord.
Amen.

All Souls
November 2

W E REJOICE IN YOU, O LORD.
We exult in your deliverance.
All of our bones declare
that there is no one like you
to deliver the weak from those who are strong,
to deliver the needy from those who despoil them.
As we remember all our dead relatives and friends,
we also rejoice in your mercy and love.
Bless our food and sharing
that they may strengthen us in your service.
We ask this through Christ our Lord. Amen.

W E TRUST IN YOU AT ALL TIMES, O GOD.
We pour out our hearts before you.
We know those of low estate are but a breath,
those of high estate are but a delusion.
All power and steadfast love belong to you.
As we remember all who have fallen asleep in Christ,
strengthen us with this food
that we might place all our trust in you.
We ask this through Christ our Lord. Amen.

Feast of the Dedication of St. John Lateran
November 9

G OD, YOU ARE A REFUGE AND STRENGTH,
a very present help in trouble,
and always with us.
We do not fear though the mountains tremble,
though the waters of the sea roar and foam.
From your church flows streams of living water.
You are in its midst and it shall not be moved.
As we celebrate the dedication of St. John Lateran,
bless our food, keep us strong,
and make us aware of your presence.
We ask this through Christ our Lord. Amen.

Feast of St. Andrew
November 30

Your eyes are upon those who revere you, O Lord;
your eyes are upon those
who hope in your steadfast love.
As we celebrate the feast of St. Andrew,
we wait for you to save us from death.
Our hearts are glad in you as we share this food
because we trust in your holy name.
Let your steadfast love be upon us,
even as we hope in you
through Jesus Christ our Lord. Amen.

Solemnity of Christ the King
Last Sunday in Ordinary Time

The Lord is God!
He is exalted among the nations.
Out of the death of his only son,
he has brought new life to all the earth
and made him the king of the universe.
May our celebration of this feast
and the food and drink we share
serve to prepare us one day to stand in his sight.
He lives and reigns forever and ever.
Amen.

O God, you have prolonged the life
of Christ our King
through the resurrection of Jesus from the grave.
May he be enthroned forever at your right side.
May your steadfast love and faithfulness watch over us
as we share this food and drink.
We praise your name
through the same Christ our Lord. Amen.

Solemnity of the Immaculate Conception
December 8

We clap our hands
and shout to you with glad songs of joy, O Lord.
You, the Most High, are awesome,
a great king over all the earth.
You prepared the Virgin of Nazareth
to be the worthy mother of your son
by wrapping her in the grace of your holiness.
As we remember her Immaculate Conception,
bless our food and drink.
All glory be to you, Father, Son, and Holy Spirit,
one God forever and ever. Amen.

Feast of Our Lady of Guadalupe
December 12

O Lord, you have been our dwelling place
in all generations.
Before the mountains were brought forth,
before you ever formed the earth and the world,
from everlasting to everlasting you are God.
You chose to reveal the mother of your son in Mexico
to shower us with your steadfast love.
As we celebrate the feast of Our Lady of Guadalupe,
make us grateful for these gifts of food and drink.
Hear our prayer through Jesus Christ, your son,
born of the Virgin Mary and Lord forever and ever.
Amen.

Solemnity of Christmas
December 25

G REAT ARE YOU, O LORD, AND HIGHLY TO BE PRAISED.
We ponder your steadfast love
as we celebrate the birth of your only-begotten son.
Your name, like your praise,
now reaches to the ends of the earth.
May our Christmas feast be acceptable to you,
serve as thanksgiving from us,
and as praise of your holy name.
We ask this through our Lord Jesus Christ,
who lives and reigns with you and the Holy Spirit,
one God, forever and ever. Amen.

Feast of St. Stephen
December 26

O Lord, in the depths of our hearts
you speak your words of wisdom.
We do not fear those who can kill the body
because there is no ransom that can save our lives.
Through his death and resurrection,
your son, Jesus Christ,
has removed the sting of death
and offered us eternal life.
As we celebrate the feast of the martyr Stephen,
crown our faithfulness with life beyond the grave.
Through this food and drink,
give us the strength to serve you all our days.
Hear us in the name of Jesus Christ our Lord. Amen.

Feast of St. John
December 27

Happy are those whom you love, O Lord,
for you teach them out of your law,
giving them respite from days of trouble
and filling them with the words of your lips.
As we celebrate this feast of St. John,
the herald of the Word-made-flesh,
grant your blessing upon this food.
Be our stronghold and rock.
We pray through Christ our Lord. Amen.

Feast of the Holy Innocents
December 28

O Lord, you are king, robed in majesty
and girded with strength.
You created the world not to be moved;
your throne is established from of old.
Through the witness of your holy innocents,
you have bathed your children in martyrdom
and given them the gift of holiness.
May our celebration of this feast
and the food and drink we share
serve to praise your majestic work.
Hear us through Christ our Lord. Amen.

Feast of the Holy Family
Sunday after Christmas or December 30

Mighty One, Lord God,
you speak and summon the earth
from the rising of the sun to its setting.
You bid us to offer you a sacrifice of thanksgiving
and to keep the promises we have made to you.
As we celebrate the feast of the Holy Family,
we honor you with this prayer of thanksgiving
for the food and drink you have set upon our table.
Bless this family and let your face shine upon us
through Jesus Christ our Lord. Amen.

O Lord, you have built this house
and you guard all those who live here.
Make our family holy
and bless this food and drink we share.
May peace always reign here.
We give you praise and thanks
through Jesus Christ our Lord. Amen.

Special Days

BIRTHDAYS

O LORD,
We have asked you for life
and you have given us length of days.
Thank you for all the rich blessings of the past years,
for giving us the joy of serving in your presence.
Deepen our trust in you,
and through your steadfast love
and the gifts of this food and drink,
give us strength to continue to walk in your ways.
Hear our prayer through Christ our Lord. Amen.

O LORD, OUR HOPE, OUR TRUST.
Upon you have we leaned from birth.
In you have we trusted from youth.
In our older years do not forsake us
when our strength is spent.
Bless this food and drink
which we use to mark another year in your service.
May we never cease to praise you
through Jesus Christ, our Lord. Amen.

YOU HAVE TAUGHT US FROM YOUTH, O GOD,
and we still proclaim your wondrous deeds.
Even with old age and gray hairs,
We continue to announce your wonders.
Through this celebration of birth,
grant that we may proclaim your might
to all the generations to come.
Hear our prayer through Christ our Lord. Amen.

WE PRAISE YOU, O LORD, AS LONG AS WE LIVE.
We sing praises to you, our God,
all our lives long.
You made the heaves and the earth,
the sea, and all that is in them.
You keep faith forever,
giving food to the hungry.
Bless this food on _____'s birthday
and continue to watch over us
all the days of our lives.
Hear this prayer of thanksgiving
through Jesus Christ our Lord. Amen.

B LESSED BE YOUR NAME, O LORD.
You are our rock, our fortress, our deliverer.
What are we human beings that you regard us,
mere mortals that you think of us?
We are like a breath;
our days like passing shadows.
Yet you bless us with many years
so that we might serve you in faithfulness
all the days of our lives.
As we celebrate the birth of _____
with this food and drink,
we make this prayer of thanksgiving
through Jesus Christ our Lord. Amen.

DURING AN ILLNESS

O GOD, DO NOT BE FAR FROM US;
O my God, make haste to help us.
We hope continually in your healing touch.
Strengthen _____ with your blessing upon this food.
We ask this through Christ our Lord. Amen.

H EAR OUR PRAYER, O LORD;
let our cries come to you.
Do not hide your face from us
in the days of our distress.
Incline your ear to us;
answer us speedily in the day when we call.
Our days pass away like smoke,
and our bones burn like a furnace.
Our hearts are stricken and withered like grass.
Bless this food before us;
may it bring health in mind and body
through Jesus Christ our Lord. Amen.

AFTER AN ILLNESS

B LESSED BE THE LORD,
for he has heard the sound of our pleas.
The Lord is our strength and our shield;
in him our hearts trust.
He has come to our help.
And so our hearts exult and with prayer
we give thanks to him for this food and drink
through Jesus Christ our Lord. Amen.

W E SING PRAISES TO YOU, O LORD,
and give thanks to your holy name.
You have favored us throughout our lives.
When we wept in the night,
you brought joy with the morning.
Bless this food and keep us in your healing care.
We ask this through Christ our Lord. Amen.

G RACIOUS ARE YOU, O LORD,
and righteous and merciful.
When we called to you, you heard our voice.
We suffered distress and anguish,
and you saved us.
Continue to deliver us from death,
our eyes from tears, our feet from stumbling.
We walk before you, O Lord, in the land of the living.
Sustain our lives with your blessing upon this food.
We ask this through Jesus Christ our Lord. Amen.

W E GIVE THANKS TO YOU, O LORD,
for you are good;
your steadfast love endures forever.
Out of our distress we called on you
and you answered us and set us free.
Make us more aware of your blessings
as we share this food and drink before you.
With you on our side to help us
we will praise your name forever and ever. Amen.

THANKSGIVING

O LORD, YOUR GOODNESS IS ABUNDANT.
Your face shines upon us.
Make us grateful for all our blessings.
Bless this food and drink
and all who gather around this table,
through Jesus Christ our Lord. Amen.

O GOD, YOU CROWN THE YEAR WITH YOUR BOUNTY;
your wagon tracks overflow with richness.
The pastures of the wilderness overflow;
the hills gird themselves with joy,
the meadows clothe themselves with flocks,
the valleys deck themselves with grain.
Make us thankful for all your gifts,
especially for this food that we are about to share.
All of us shout and sing your praises joyfully
through Christ our Lord. Amen.

WE GIVE YOU THANKS, O LORD,
WITH OUR WHOLE HEARTS.
We sing your praise before the whole world.
We thank you for your steadfast love and faithfulness.
Your right hand feeds us and sustains us.
We bow to your exalted name, O Lord,
for your word gives us life
and helps us to walk in your ways.
All glory be to you now and forever. Amen.

With a Friend

O LORD, YOU KNOW THE SECRETS OF OUR HEARTS.
Bless this food and time we spend together.
We know that where two of us are gathered
in your name
you are always present.
Be a guest at our table
and hear our prayer
through Christ our Lord. Amen.

After a Hard Day

O LORD,
this day is like a dream in your sight.
As quickly as it began it has come to an end.
Teach us to count all our days
so that we may gain a wise heart.
As you bless this food you set before us,
send your favor upon us
and prosper the work of our hands.
We ask this through Christ our Lord. Amen.

O LORD, WE CRY TO YOU IN OUR NEED
and you promise to save us from our distress.
Bring us out of darkness and gloom,
and we will thank you for your steadfast love.
Hear our prayer through Jesus Christ our Lord. Amen.

G UARD US, O LORD, FROM THE HANDS OF THE WICKED;
protect us from the violent and the arrogant.
You are our God, our strong deliverer.
Bless this food and drink
as we give thanks to your holy name,
now and forever and ever. Amen.

Celebrating Forgiveness

O LORD, GOD OF ALL,
    forever you keep your steadfast love with us
even when we fail and break your covenant.
We come before you confessing our sins
and we have known
the unlimited forgiveness you promise.
Use this food and drink to keep us faithful.
You are our Father, our God,
and the Rock of our salvation.
We offer you praise and thanks
through Christ our Lord. Amen.

Mother's Day

W E CALL UPON YOU, O LORD;
come quickly to us;
give ear to our voices when we call to you.
Hold us close to you with compassion and kindness,
like a mother holds her children to her bosom.
Bless this food and drink
with which we celebrate mother's day.
Bless our mother and keep her close to you
through Jesus Christ our Lord. Amen.

Father's Day

L OVING AND MERCIFUL GOD,
you have compassion on us
like a father who loves his children.
You know that we are made of dust;
we flourish like the flower of the fields
and then we are gone.
Bless this food and drink
which we use to celebrate Father's Day.
Bless our father and keep him close to you
through Jesus Christ our Lord. Amen.

After a Quiet Day

O Lord, our hearts are stilled
and our eyes are lowered.
We have not occupied ourselves
with things too great for us.
See our calm and quiet souls,
which are like a weaned child on a mother's lap,
and bless this simple meal.
All our hope is placed in you
from this time on and forevermore. Amen.

O Lord, you have chosen to live within those
who follow your ways.
We praise you for your abundant provisions,
for bread for the poor, for salvation for all.
Come and rest in us
as we share this meal together.
Hear us through Christ our Lord. Amen.

Also Available

PRAYERS FOR SLEEPLESS NIGHTS
Helen Reichert Lambin

This original collection of prayers focuses on those topics of stress, tension, and frustration that keep us up at night and provides a framework to do something constructive during those lost hours of sleep: create a personal, prayerful relationship with God.

80 pages, paperback, $12.95

INTERCESSIONS OF MERCY

This inspirational prayer volume offers a practical approach to petitioning God's help and provision on behalf of family members, friends, colleagues, community and business leaders, and the less fortunate around the world. Designed for individuals and group settings, *Intercessions of Mercy* journeys through the liturgical cycle of seasons and feasts.

360 pages, paperback, $19.95

A CONTEMPORARY CELTIC PRAYER BOOK

This beautiful prayer book captures the flavor of traditional Celtic spirituality with a simplified Liturgy of the Hours and a treasury of Celtic prayers, blessings and rituals.

160 pages, paperback, $9.95

A CONTEMPORARY NORTH AMERICAN PRAYER BOOK

This prayer book is both "Contemporary" and "North American." It is contemporary because it tries to use current and inclusive language whenever possible, in ways that reflect the usage of people today. It is North American because it uses the places, persons and history of North America as a basis for prayer and meditation.

160 pages, paperback, $12.95

Available from booksellers
or from ACTA Publications, www.actapublications.com